D1277640

Cover Photograph
The two types of vitamin capsules
displayed on the front cover are the
conventional brown shaded Vitamin E
capsules and the new clear Natural Factors
Vitamin E pills which encapsulate the Clear
Base form of the vitamin.

*This book has been printed solely on recycled
paper to help conserve our environment.*

> *A SIMPLIFIED, FULLY ILLUSTRATED TEXT WHICH MAKES UNDERSTANDING CHOLESTEROL AND HEART DISEASE EASY AND FAST!*

ANTIOXIDANTS, CHOLESTEROL & HEART DISEASE

HOW VITAMIN E AND ANTIOXIDANTS MAY HELP YOU

LIFE CYCLE PUBLISHING

Grant N. Pierce, Ph.D.

Bram Ramjiawan, B.Sc.

Antioxidants, Cholesterol & Heart Disease

ANTIOXIDANTS, CHOLESTEROL & HEART DISEASE

Grant N. Pierce
St. Boniface General Hospital Research Centre

Bram Ramjiawan
National Research Council Institute for Biodiagnostics

ABOUT THE AUTHORS

Dr. Grant N. Pierce received his graduate training from Dalhousie University and the University of Manitoba. After receiving his Ph.D. degree in Physiology, he carried out his postdoctoral studies in Los Angeles at UCLA. Dr. Pierce then returned to the University of Manitoba where he is currently Professor in the Department of Physiology, Faculty of Medicine, and in the Division of Cardiovascular Sciences, St. Boniface General Hospital Research Centre, Winnipeg, Canada. Dr. Pierce has received a number of prestigious national and international awards for his research in heart disease. He has published over 80 research papers and written or edited three books on the topic of heart disease. He is currently the Assistant Editor of the journal <u>Molecular and Cellular Biochemistry</u> and a member of the Editorial Boards of <u>Circulation Research</u> and the <u>Journal of Molecular and Cellular Cardiology</u>. Dr Pierce was recently elected as a Council Member of the American Section of the International Society for Heart Research.

Bram Ramjiawan completed his B.Sc. degree at the University of Winnipeg before going on to graduate study. He is currently nearing completion of his M.Sc. degree in the Department of Physiology, Faculty of Medicine at the University of Manitoba. He has published a number of full length research papers in scientific journals. Mr. Ramjiawan also has about a decade of experience working in the health food industry. He is presently employed in the Surgical Section of the Institute for Biodiagnostics, National Research Council of Canada, Winnipeg.

LIFE CYCLE PUBLISHING

194 Foxmeadow Drive, Winnipeg, Manitoba, Canada R3P 1T3

This book represents information obtained from highly regarded and authentic sources. Every reasonable effort has been made to give reliable data and information but the authors and publisher cannot assume responsibility for the validity of all of the materials or for the consequences of their use.

ISBN # 0-9699096-0-8

Printed in Canada.

Antioxidants, Cholesterol & Heart Disease

<u>DEDICATION</u>

This book is dedicated with love to our parents who gave us life and continually nurtured and guided us both physically and spiritually throughout their lives.

PREFACE

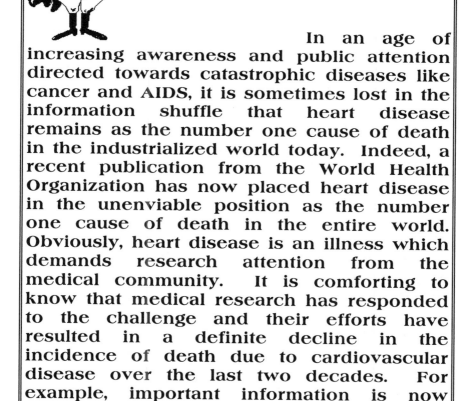

Preeeesenting...

In an age of increasing awareness and public attention directed towards catastrophic diseases like cancer and AIDS, it is sometimes lost in the information shuffle that heart disease remains as the number one cause of death in the industrialized world today. Indeed, a recent publication from the World Health Organization has now placed heart disease in the unenviable position as the number one cause of death in the entire world. Obviously, heart disease is an illness which demands research attention from the medical community. It is comforting to know that medical research has responded to the challenge and their efforts have resulted in a definite decline in the incidence of death due to cardiovascular disease over the last two decades. For example, important information is now available to the public on how diet and exercise may help in the fight against heart failure. These therapies are so important and so powerful as tools to fight heart disease that the general public cannot afford to ignore them. Knowledge of the significance of cholesterol as a risk factor for heart disease is now considered by experts in the area to be critical for modifying, delaying and even preventing the occurrence of complications associated with coronary artery disease. The purpose of this book is to provide the reader with an update about how cholesterol wreaks such havoc in the body and what we may be able to do to avoid this damage. It is written with a special emphasis on making the language and terms as simple and easily understandable as possible. This is not a medical text for the medical student. It is an informative reference text for the general public which we believe will be "reader-friendly" and not confused with medical jargon and scientific terms known only to scientists in the field. Basic information is presented to help the reader understand exactly what is a "heart attack" or a "stroke" or "good" versus "bad" cholesterol. At the same time, every effort has been made to present the latest advances in the area so that the reader is educated as best as possible. To this end, one of the focuses of the book concerns the role of antioxidants in heart disease. The role of antioxidants as agents to combat heart disease is a new field of research which is rapidly evolving. Current information supports their efficacy as agents to protect against arterial disease in the heart. While some of the public does appear to know generally that antioxidants like vitamin E may be helpful in the fight against heart disease, it is a minority of the population. More people need to be aware of the potential benefits of antioxidant therapy. Furthermore, even those who do know of the potential benefits of antioxidant usage are not generally aware of why or how the antioxidants work. This book presents the first detailed information available to the public on the topic of antioxidants and their interactions with cholesterol in heart disease. The book details how oxidative processes interact with cholesterol in the body to block critical arteries feeding the heart with energy. Information is also included describing the cholesterol and antioxidant content of various foods. Thus, every effort has been made to provide an informative, easy-to-understand text which covers everything from the known risk factors for heart disease to the mechanisms whereby arteries are plugged by cholesterol deposits, to dietary modifications which are recommended to improve your health. The book has been complimented with many illustrations to further its appeal and readability. We hope that the text succeeds in its objective of providing an informative treatise of antioxidants, cholesterol and heart disease in a fun, easily understood, illustrated manner.

Grant N. Pierce, Ph.D.
Bram Ramjiawan, B.Sc.

ACKNOWLEDGEMENTS

The creation of a book does not occur through the isolated efforts of just the co-authors. We would like to thank first and foremost, our wives, Gail and Fatima, who have been great sources of support, inspiration and help during the writing of this book. We would like to acknowledge the fine artwork, layout design and photography of Mr. Bill Peters on the cover. We would also like to thank our colleagues in the lab here and all over the world who work tirelessly to find answers to the difficult questions facing them in cardiovascular disease. Lastly, we would like to thank those who have supported our research efforts now and in the past: the Medical Research Council, the Heart and Stroke Foundation, the National Research Council and the St. Boniface General Hospital Research Foundation. Without their help, we would not be able to make any progress into the mechanisms underlying a

Antioxidants, Cholesterol & Heart Disease

disease which ends more lives than any
other.

CONTENTS

PART I

THE BASICS: What Enquiring Minds Need To Know About Cholesterol And Heart Disease

Antioxidants, Cholesterol & Heart Disease

CHAPTER 1

CHOLESTEROL

CHAPTER 2

HEART DISEASE

Antioxidants, Cholesterol & Heart Disease

PART II

THE LATEST INFO: The Antioxidant Defence Against Heart Disease

Antioxidants, Cholesterol & Heart Disease

CHAPTER 3

OXIDIZED LDL

How does cholesterol (or LDL) produce a blockage in an artery?..66

How does LDL become oxidized?..70

Antioxidants, Cholesterol & Heart Disease

CHAPTER 4

ANTIOXIDANTS
AND LDL

PART III

PREVENTION: Fighting The Good Fight Against Cholesterol And Heart Disease

Antioxidants, Cholesterol & Heart Disease

CHAPTER 5

<u>LOWERING YOUR CHOLESTEROL LEVELS</u>

I have a friend who exercised regularly, ate carefully, and still died from a heart attack. Why should I follow such a life style if it doesn't work?..87

If I am successful in lowering my blood cholesterol, can I reverse the heart disease or are the blockages in my arteries permanent?..89

I carefully choose foods low in cholesterol but I can't seem to lower my blood cholesterol concentration.   Why can't I?..91

Antioxidants, Cholesterol & Heart Disease

CHAPTER 6

OTHER IMPORTANT STRATEGIES TO REGULATE CHOLESTEROL

Are there any drugs available which will lower my blood cholesterol concentration? How do they work and are there any side-effects?..96

What are polyunsaturated fats and why are they good for us?..102

If I increase the fiber content of my diet, will it reduce my chances of having a heart attack?.105

Is exercise important?..107

Antioxidants, Cholesterol & Heart Disease

CHAPTER 7

NUTRITIONAL ADVICE

APPENDIX *..141*

INDEX *..142*

THE BASICS:
WHAT ENQUIRING MINDS
NEED TO KNOW ABOUT
CHOLESTEROL AND
HEART DISEASE

CHAPTER 1:

CHOLESTEROL

WHAT IS CHOLESTEROL?

There are many types of fats in the body. Cholesterol is one particular type of fat (another name for fat is lipid).

Antioxidants, Cholesterol & Heart Disease

Cholesterol is absolutely essential for the proper functioning of your body. For example, it is an important constituent in the synthesis of steroid hormones in the body. These hormones are critical factors in determining many female characteristics in a woman. For example, follicle stimulating hormone and leutinizing hormone are factors only produced in women and are involved in initiating and terminating the menstrual cycle and various aspects surrounding pregnancy. Other steroid hormones are crucial in determining the male characteristics in men. For example, testosterone is an important hormone in producing the characteristic changes which occur during the transformation of a boy into a man during pubescence/adolescence. However, cholesterol is even more important because of the structural role it plays in virtually every cell in the body. Our body is composed of many different organ systems: the heart, the brain, the lungs and the liver just to name a few. Each one of these organs is composed at a much smaller level of millions of tiny cells. It is these cells which are the working units of the organ. Each cell will work in concert with another to perform a specific function. For example, in the heart, all the cells will contract in unison: the end result is that the heart as a whole will pump blood to the rest of the body. For the cell to perform its function properly, it must

be separated from the fluid surrounding it.
Much like the rubber of a balloon forms a
barrier separating the air inside the balloon
from the air outside the balloon,

the cell also has a
specialized sheath or membrane
surrounding it which allows it to create a
special environment within the cell which is
quite unique and distinct from that on the
outside of the cell. Without a viable, intact
cell membrane on its surface, the cell will
die. Fats are the primary component of this
cell wall and cholesterol is one of the types
of fats found here. Cholesterol provides
structural rigidity to the surface membrane
and also influences the function of the cell.
Without cholesterol, cell function and
viability throughout most organs in the body
would become compromised. Ultimately, if
organ function becomes abnormal, our body

function will be abnormal. Cholesterol, therefore, is a fat which is absolutely essential for the body to have in appropriate amounts if the body is to perform properly.

DO ALL LIVING ORGANISMS CONTAIN CHOLESTEROL?

No. It is a common misconception, for example, that plants contain cholesterol. All plants contain sitosterol which is a type of fat that is structurally similar to cholesterol but, fortunately for us, is broken down in our bodies very differently than cholesterol. Even though sitosterol and cholesterol are related, ingestion of plant material will not raise cholesterol levels in humans. (Please see Chapter 5 for some important qualifications to this general rule). Animals and humans do contain cholesterol. There are two sources for this cholesterol in our body. First, our bodies make cholesterol naturally. Most of the cells in the body are capable of synthesizing moderate quantities of cholesterol. Second, we can eat material which contains cholesterol. Ingestion of any animal products that contain cholesterol (fish and poultry products contain cholesterol too) will ultimately result in some of the cholesterol contained in that meat to become absorbed into our blood stream and deposited within our bodies as well. Because our bodies make their own cholesterol naturally anyway, we require relatively little cholesterol from our diet to meet the needs of the body.

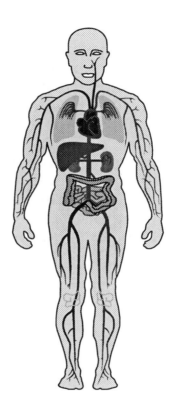

IF CHOLESTEROL IS SO IMPORTANT TO THE BODY, WHY DO DOCTORS WARN US AGAINST IT?

As discussed above, it is true that cholesterol is an important fat for the body. We require it. It is also true that cholesterol is a dangerous fat to have in our body. We'll discuss precisely why this is the case later in the book. However, suffice it to say here that the critical factor in this apparent paradox is the quantity or concentration of cholesterol. This will determine whether it will be beneficial or harmful to the body. Cholesterol in modest, appropriate amounts is helpful to maintain the proper function of your body. It is only when cholesterol levels reach abnormally high concentrations that it begins to have effects on the body which can be catastrophic if unattended.

Antioxidants, Cholesterol & Heart Disease

WHY IS CHOLESTEROL HARMFUL TO THE BODY?

As indicated previously, excessively high concentrations of cholesterol in the blood can cause serious health problems. Occasionally, one can read reports in the news that blood cholesterol levels are not harmful to you or that other factors may be responsible for heart disease. Although it is true that a high circulating level of cholesterol in the blood is not the only risk factor associated with heart disease, it is clear from the overwhelming majority of scientific studies that blood cholesterol levels are the strongest independent prognosticator for heart disease. While individual small studies may create sensational headlines by challenging the cholesterol/heart disease association, one must always be keenly aware that there are probably 50 studies showing the strongest relationship between cholesterol and heart disease for every one which does not.

Furthermore, the studies demonstrating the importance of blood cholesterol as a risk factor in heart disease have been huge studies involving as many as hundreds of thousands of patients. They have been carried on over many years and even decades, and they have been initiated and have had their data collected from countries all over the world. The association of cholesterol with heart disease is not a casual relationship peculiar to one part of the globe or one particular race of people. All people are affected by this strong association. The association of cholesterol with heart disease is not only an American problem: it is now a global one. Whereas we used to refer to cardiovascular disease as the leading cause of death in industrialized countries, the World Health Organization recently named cardiovascular disease as the number one killer in the entire world. The association of cholesterol with heart disease is so powerful that Dr. William C. Roberts, Editor-In-Chief of the American Journal of Cardiology recently predicted in a 1993 publication that the greatest potential agent in the fight against heart failure will be a lipid lowering agent. This underlines the critical importance of cholesterol as an independent risk factor in heart disease. The bottom line is: if you can control your blood cholesterol levels within acceptable guidelines, you will be doing one of the most important things you can to reduce your chances of suffering from cardiovascular disease.

WHAT IS AN ACCEPTABLE BLOOD CHOLESTEROL CONCENTRATION? WHAT IS A DANGEROUS LEVEL?

SERUM CHOLESTEROL

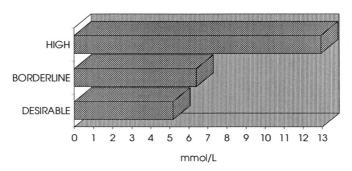

mmol/L

Testing for cholesterol starts with a nurse taking a small blood sample from a vein in your arm. The clinical biochemistry laboratory within the hospital will then complete a test to measure the total serum cholesterol level or to measure the cholesterol level in the LDL fraction. Blood (or serum) levels of cholesterol were categorized by the United States National Cholesterol Education Program into desirable, borderline risk, and high cholesterol groups.

Antioxidants, Cholesterol & Heart Disease

Desirable total cholesterol levels in the serum are less than 200 mg/dl. Borderline high cholesterol concentration is 200-240 mg/dl. High serum total cholesterol is greater than 240 mg/dl. Serum LDL cholesterol levels of less than 130 mg/dl are considered desirable, 130-160 mg/dl are borderline high risk, 160-190 mg/dl are high risk and greater than 190 mg/dl are very high risk levels of serum LDL cholesterol. Depending upon the country or even the hospital, the units for measuring cholesterol may be reported as mg/dl or mM.

TOTAL SERUM CHOLESTEROL

UNITS	DESIRABLE	BORDERLINE-HIGH	HIGH
mmol/L	5.17	5.17-6.21	Greater than 6.21
mg/dL	200	200-240	Greater than 240

LDL SERUM CHOLESTEROL

UNITS	DESIRABLE	BORDERLINE-HIGH	HIGH	VERY HIGH
mmol/L	Less than 3.36	3.36-4.14	4.14-4.91	Greater than 4.91
mg/dL	Less than 130	130-160	160-190	Greater than 190

I HAVE OFTEN HEARD THE TERMS "GOOD" AND "BAD" CHOLESTEROL USED. WHAT DO THEY MEAN?

Cholesterol is a fat. Like most other fats, cholesterol does not associate well with water or most aqueous mediums. Oil, which another type of fat, is a good example of this property. Pour any type of cooking oil commonly used in the kitchen into a glass containing water and you will see that the oil does not dissolve but instead accumulates on the water's surface. The oil does not "like" being in the water and repels the water to form tiny balls on the surface rather than directly associate with the water in a dissolved state. Cholesterol exhibits similar properties when immersed into water or blood. Thus, it cannot be transported by blood in this state. To help in transforming the cholesterol into a compound which is more easily transported in the blood to the cells which require it, the cholesterol is combined with other fats and one or more specific proteins. The most important type of fat/protein combination is called low density lipoprotein or LDL for short. LDL is the primary carrier of cholesterol in the blood. So, for all intents and purposes here, when one refers to cholesterol in the blood, they are actually referring to LDL. LDL is responsible for taking cholesterol from the liver (which is the primary organ in the body for making LDL and breaking down LDL) and transporting it in the blood stream all over the body. It is intimately involved therefore in the process of heart disease because of its capacity to deposit cholesterol in the arteries. It is not at all surprising, therefore, that LDL has a strong positive correlation with heart disease similar to cholesterol's association with heart disease. Because of this relationship, LDL has been called "bad" cholesterol.

Fats are also carried in the blood with other kinds of proteins. Another particular kind of lipoprotein which is different than LDL is called high density lipoprotein or HDL. HDL has less fat associated with it than LDL. Its job in the circulation is the opposite of the LDL or bad cholesterol. HDL functions to take cholesterol away from the tissues and organs of the body. Therefore, it functions as a kind of anti-atherosclerotic agent aiding in the general process of removing cholesterol from the body. Again, not surprisingly, it has a strong relationship with heart disease. Except this time the relationship is such that if you have a high concentration of HDL in the blood, you have a lesser risk of incurring heart disease than someone who may have low HDL concentrations. That's exactly the opposite

Antioxidants, Cholesterol & Heart Disease

of LDL where high concentrations of it will increase your likelihood of heart disease. Because of this inverse relationship with heart disease, HDL has been called "good cholesterol". Normally, the cost of measuring HDL levels in the blood is too high for routine testing in all people. Usually, HDL measurements are only carried out in medical studies or in patients with suspected heart problems. It would be beneficial in the future to incorporate routine analysis of blood HDL concentration during a clinical cardiovascular evaluation of a patient. However, this will probably await the development of more economical ways of detecting HDL than currently exist today.

Antioxidants, Cholesterol & Heart Disease

IF I HAVE HIGH BLOOD CHOLESTEROL LEVELS, AM I DOOMED TO A PREMATURE DEATH?

Certainly not, and for several reasons. First, although the association of cholesterol with heart disease is strong, it is not absolute. Some people seem to be able to withstand high circulating levels of cholesterol without suffering from any of the major complications of heart disease. Statistically, however, everyone's chances are better if cholesterol is reduced. Secondly, blood cholesterol levels can be changed. It is only reasonable to believe that if one can dramatically raise blood cholesterol levels by eating fatty meats, then restraining from these foods should reduce blood cholesterol concentrations just as well. Scientific data does appear to support this hypothesis and we will discuss this important issue in greater detail later in the book (see Part III). Thirdly, as we alluded to earlier, although cholesterol is a major risk factor for predicting the occurrence of heart disease, it is not the only one. Removing other risk factors from your life will have a significant impact upon the likelihood of having a heart attack or some other form of

Antioxidants, Cholesterol & Heart Disease

heart disease. (Of course, the converse is also true! A low level of blood cholesterol does not give an iron clad guarantee that heart disease will not strike. A prudent approach would be to reduce as many of the correctable risk factors as possible.)

Antioxidants, Cholesterol & Heart Disease

CHAPTER 2:

HEART DISEASE

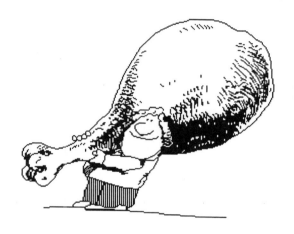

WHAT ARE THE RISK FACTORS FOR HEART DISEASE?

The primary risk factor for heart disease is a high circulating level of cholesterol in the blood.

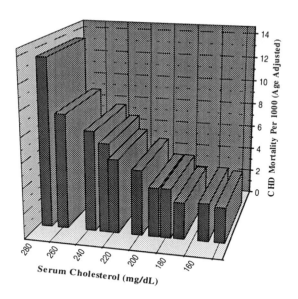

A direct relationship between serum cholesterol and coronary heart disease (CHD) exists. As shown above, when serum cholesterol levels increase there is an according increase in the incidence of mortality. Other abnormal fat patterns such as elevated triglycerides or metabolism in the blood are also important risk factors.

In addition to fats, there are still quite a number of significant risk factors which have an influence on the appearance of heart disease. These include diabetes, hypertension, cigarette smoking, obesity, age, sex and genetics. These risk factors independently affect the probability of suffering a heart attack; combined, however, they potentiate the likelihood of the dangers of heart disease. The graph below shows the effects of increased cholesterol levels on the incidence of coronary heart disease in the presence of other risk factors. Consider, for example, a 50-year-old male with high cholesterol, but no other risk factors. Another male, again 50 years of age and with the same condition, but also has a history of smoking, high blood pressure and is obese. The probability of this individual suffering complications related to heart disease are considerably higher than that of the first individual.

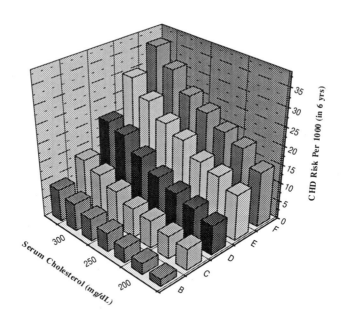

B - INCREASING CHOLESTEROL
C - INCREASING CHOLESTEROL PLUS HIGH
BLOOD PRESSURE
D - INCREASING CHOLESTEROL PLUS HIGH
BLOOD SUGAR
E - INCREASING CHOLESTEROL PLUS SMOKING
F - INCREASING CHOLESTEROL PLUS LOW HDL

Diabetes mellitus and its inherent condition of abnormal blood sugar concentrations is another important, independent risk factor in heart disease. To date but four general areas have been identified as potentially important. First, diabetic patients appear to have an accelerated atherogenic plaque development in their arteries which will predispose them to more frequent heart attacks. Second, they also have blockages and defects in their small sized vessels which may hinder how foods needed for energy may be transported to the working cells. Third, there appears to be a number of defects in the working cells of the heart which compromise their ability to contract properly and, therefore, ultimately reduce the efficiency of the heart as a pump per se. Finally, some diabetic patients have neural disorders which may significantly increase their pain threshold. These patients may experience a heart attack without feeling the characteristic pain associated with it. This will greatly increase the amount of time that these patients take before seeking medical help. This delay in reaching medical assistance will reduce their chances of survival from the heart attack or increase the damage caused by the coronary episode.

Cigarette smoking is another important risk factor. Precisely why smoking increases our chances of having a heart attack is not entirely clear but recent data suggests that it may have something to do with an important modification of LDL in the blood which makes it more dangerous to us (for more information refer to Chapter 4).

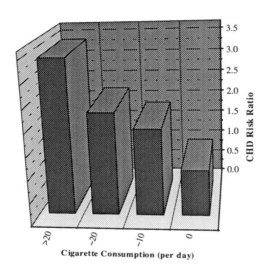

Cigarette Consumption (per day)

This graph shows the relationship between cigarette consumption (per day) and coronary risk ratio. As can be seen, there is a positive correlation between the number of cigarettes smoked per day and the likelihood of developing heart disease.

Second hand smoke can also contribute to the risk for heart disease. A recent study in the Journal of the American College of Cardiology estimated that second hand smoke will cause 47,000 deaths and about 150,000 non-fatal heart attacks in 1994 alone in the United States.

Physical inactivity and obesity are also risk factors. There is some controversy as to whether each of these items may be risk factors on their own or whether the two

are the same. However, for our purposes in real life, it is exceedingly clear that a life of inactivity leading to excessive weight gain will present an important stress to the cardiovascular system which may lead to a serious coronary event. After all, it only makes sense: if you ask your heart to pump blood to the additional miles and miles of vessels which twist and turn throughout fat deposits which need not be there, eventually the heart will get tired from all the extra work and ask for a holiday. The only problem with this is that when your heart asks for a holiday, it's usually permanent.

Stress is another well publicized risk factor for heart disease. Those who are constantly under stress either at their job or elsewhere are at greater risk to succumb to some kind of vascular event (heart attack, stroke). It has also been suggested that some individuals with inherently intense personalities (Type A) are at greater risk to have a heart attack. They are usually very ambitious, energetic, and find themselves in jobs that demand a great deal of responsibity. These people are always pushing the limits of their own physical tolerance at their job, at their home, even in their personal life. It is unclear why stress may produce heart attacks more frequently but the most common hypothesis has to do with the effects that a constant release of adrenalin may have on the body (as is thought to occur in these individuals).

The sex of a person is also a risk factor for heart disease. Please don't confuse this with the act of sex as being a risk factor for heart disease! As far as we know, sex is not a stimulus for heart failure in a healthy individual (it may be the opposite!). What we do mean, though, is that males are far more susceptible to heart disease than females. The reason for this was originally thought to be due to the different sex hormones which circulate in the bodies of the two sexes. Some evidence does appear to support this contention and hormonal replacement therapy in post menopausal women is being encouraged in some cases.

Another hypothesis that has been advanced was that the traditionally different lifestyles of men and women may account for the differences in the severity of the cardiovascular disease. It was thought that as women became more and more involved in the work place in the 21st century, their relative resistance to heart problems may gradually disappear. This has yet to be convincingly demonstrated.

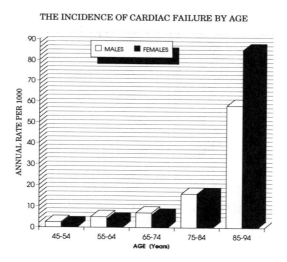

Time itself is another cardiovascular risk factor. The older one gets, the greater the statistical possibility that he or she will suffer from a coronary or cerebrovascular event (heart attack or stroke).

THE INCIDENCE OF CARDIAC FAILURE BY AGE

Likely, the chronic bombardment of other risk factors upon the vessels in the body eventually weakens them to the point where finally, at some point in time, the body no longer has the capacity to resist and the straw that broke the camel's heart gives way and a heart attack ensues.

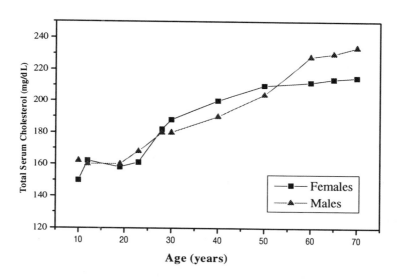

Finally, genetics is an important risk factor for heart disease in all individuals. This is one risk factor that is not correctable at present. We are a product of our mother's and father's gene banks and, fortunately or unfortunately, we're stuck with it. This accounts for the variability in heart disease from one individual to another. How often have you heard someone say "Harold eats a ton of all the wrong foods and still has a normal blood cholesterol level and I just look at ice cream and my cholesterol concentration goes through the roof!"? Genetic make-up is the source of the frustration here and it can play with our minds. Genetics tricks us and fools us at every turn. For example, because of the individual differences which exist with respect to everyone's susceptibility to heart disease, we all, deep down, like to believe that we are the ones with the good genes. We are the invincible Samsons who can down hamburgers, ice cream and fatty foods without a care for the consequences. Because, after all, until proven otherwise, we have been blessed with the resistant genes. It is only when the warning signs appear (high blood cholesterol levels or worse, black-out spells, chest pain or loss of breath) that we begin to acknowledge that maybe we aren't as immortal as we had originally hoped. The problem is that by this time, your divine revelation may have come too late. It is always better to play it safe than sorry. Statistical data tells us what the chances of having a heart attack are in a large population of people. To some extent, that removes the influence of individual genetics. Carefully consider these risk factors and then let nature take its own course with respect to your own genetic make-up. Don't play the fool and tempt the fates. No one has a crystal ball to look into the future of your heart. Your genes may make you more resistant to heart disease,

I SEE A LONG, HEALTHY LIFE FOR YOU AND YOUR HEART!

but then again, they may not. Why take the chance with your heart? On the positive side, molecular biologists are now beginning to understand the genes which may pre-dispose some individuals to heart failure. We are on the scientific verge of major break throughs in gene therapy where individuals may have defects in their genetic material corrected to prevent or delay the progression of significant cardiovascular complications. The time is not here yet for this technology to benefit most of us. However, with the help of dedicated, hard working scientists studying this technique in animals, the day will soon come when gene therapy will be a crucial clinical tool to help our children fight heart disease.

PRECISELY WHY IS CHOLESTEROL (OR LDL) BAD FOR THE BODY? WHY DOES IT CAUSE HEART DISEASE?

The primary reason why cholesterol has such a bad reputation and such a good relationship with heart disease is because of what it does in the arteries of your body. Blood is pumped out of your heart through your arteries to all parts of the body. The blood carries nutrients to the working tissue cells to allow them to continue their job and also takes away all the waste material. As discussed previously, one of those nutrients that the blood carries to the tissues is cholesterol in the form of LDL. Normally, LDL will attach to specific proteins called LDL "receptors" which are located on the cell surface. The LDL is then taken up into the cell and used for various purposes within the cell. However, if the cell does not have any receptors or has reduced the number of these receptors on the cell surface, the LDL can no longer enter the cell. Thus, it will remain in the blood. Eventually, if this occurs enough throughout the body, LDL will gain reduced entry to all tissues of the body and this will result in the backing up of LDL in the arteries. This will cause

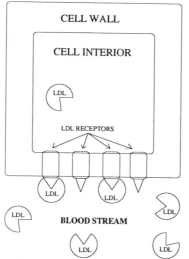

Receptors for LDL which are imbedded in the cell wall bind LDL as it floats by and take it up inside the cell.

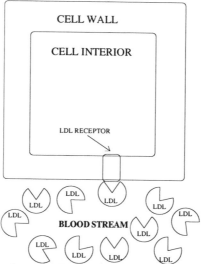

A cell which lacks the LDL receptor or has less of the receptors will not take up as much LDL from the blood. The result will be a much higher LDL concentration (and cholesterol level) found in the bloodstream.

Antioxidants, Cholesterol & Heart Disease

higher than normal LDL levels in the blood. The LDL will then accumulate on the inner surface of the arteries. It starts as a fatty streak lining the inner surface of the vessel. This appears to occur in most people at a very early age (5-10 years old!). Eventually, with time and continual exposure to high circulating LDL levels, the fatty streak builds up, higher and higher. It becomes more advanced and complicated with time. Calcium, an important element found in bones, begins to deposit in large amounts on this "growth" (thus, the term: "hardening of the arteries"). Cholesterol remains the primary constituent of the lesion, thus, the reason for its significance in heart disease. However, as the "growth" gets larger, other blood clotting factors can attach as well. The "growth" is no longer a fatty streak and is now advanced to a point where it is called a "plaque". This whole process of a blockage accumulating in an artery is termed "atherosclerosis".

The atherosclerotic plaque can block up the artery so effectively as to significantly reduce the flow of blood through it. This is not good for us because our working cells rely on the blood to bring them nutrients to maintain their function. Fortunately for us, it requires a large blockage in the arteries supplying the heart (they are called coronary arteries) before we feel the functional consequences. Amazingly, the coronary artery can be plugged up by an advanced atherosclerotic plaque by up to 70% and we still wouldn't know it. It takes a blockage of the artery of the order of greater than 80% occlusion before one begins to experience one of the most common indicators of heart vessel disease: chest pain. This is a good news/bad news scenario. It's good because it gives us a great deal of safety space where we can accumulate cholesterol in the vessel and block it up without any clinical consequences. It's bad because when the clinical problems like chest pain do appear, we now have a rather huge blockage to deal with. Chest pain is not the only clinical event which follows significant blockage of the coronary arteries. Abnormal beating patterns in the heart may also appear. These are commonly called "arrhythmias". This abnormal beating rate can compromise the ability of the heart to pump out blood to the body which, of course, ultimately means that the body's working cells will have less energy to perform their functions. The heart itself, if the coronary arteries are blocked, will not receive any energy to sustain its own pumping function and the result is a heart attack. Cholesterol and LDL is a critical factor in the development of the atherosclerotic plaque. That is why these factors have such an important association with heart disease.

WHAT IS A HEART ATTACK?

Your heart is a muscle. Its function is to pump blood out to the rest of the body. It does this by contracting all of its muscle cells in unison much like any other muscle in the body. Contraction takes energy. Anyone who has gone through a weight lifting session knows that muscle contraction is tiring! The heart is no exception. The only difference is that the heart must contract to pump that blood 60-80 times per minute over and over again for decades (we hope). It absolutely requires a large amount of energy to perform this work and it requires this energy constantly. When your muscle is contracting at such a regular rate over and over again, there had better not be any interruption in the supply of nutrients to those muscle cells to support that contractile activity. The heart has its own special arteries to provide it with the blood and nutrients necessary to complete this work. These arteries are called the

Antioxidants, Cholesterol & Heart Disease

coronary arteries. There are many of them that branch off all over the heart. The large number of arteries is required because there are so many working muscle cells in the heart which require nutrients to function. If one or more arteries get blocked for whatever reason, the heart muscle cells normally provided with blood and the necessary nutrients from that artery lose their energy to perform work very quickly. If this condition continues long enough, the cells eventually lose their ability to maintain their own biochemical life support systems and they will die. Essentially, a heart attack is an event in which the heart can no longer maintain its own integrity due to an insufficient blood flow to it and part of it dies. It does not regenerate after it is dead. Some cells in the body like the skin cells can regenerate, fix themselves and in a few weeks, you'd never know that you had a cut or a burn. Heart muscle cells are very different. Once they are dead, the event is final. The remaining heart muscle cells must take up the extra load of pumping upon themselves. If the damage is minimal, then the heart can adapt and function for days, weeks, months or years. But if the amount of dead tissue is very large, the heart will not be able to continue pumping blood and it will fail immediately. Death of the individual will be immediate as well. The survival of the patient after a heart attack is closely related to how much tissue was destroyed during the attack. If a great number of the working heart cells remain in good shape, then the patient has a good chance to survive for a relatively long period of time. Unfortunately, the converse is also true. The amount of tissue in the heart which dies will be dependent upon how big the original blockage was in the artery of the heart and how many cells to which this particular blocked artery provided nutrients. If the occluded vessel was a minor one which didn't supply many cells with nutrients, then the damage will be minor. If, however, the blockage in the coronary artery is large, or the vessel is a major one, or if more than one vessel is involved, then the damage will be more severe as will the problems in recovering from the heart attack. This entire process of artery blockage leading to compromised cell function and then cell death in the heart is called a heart attack. The individual experiencing a heart attack is probably only aware of the intense chest pain at the time of the attack. This occurs as a function of the injury to the heart muscle cells. Your physician may also refer to a heart attack as a coronary event or a myocardial infarction. The terms are synonymous with the more commonly used lay term "heart attack".

WHAT IS A STROKE?

There are two general types of strokes. Both involve a lesion in blood flow to the brain that results in death or injury to cells in the brain. In one kind of stroke, the cause is almost identical to what happens during a heart attack. In a heart attack, an atherosclerotic blockage stops blood flow to heart cells and these cells eventually become injured or die. In the brain, a blockage in an artery supplying nutrients to brain cells results in those cells dying. This is the most common type of stroke. The blockage can be caused by an atherosclerotic plaque or by a clot breaking off from a plaque elsewhere in the circulation and being lodged in a brain artery such that that artery is now blocked. The blockage can cause a temporary loss of consciousness or, if severe, permanent damage to the brain. In a second type of stroke, the artery itself will rupture due to a weakening in the arterial wall. This is called a "hemorrhagic" stroke. If the tear in the vessel wall is large enough, blood will flow out of the artery in large volumes and the results can be life threatening. This is a very difficult type of stroke for a clinician to treat immediately.

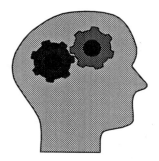

PART II

THE LATEST INFO: THE ANTIOXIDANT DEFENCE AGAINST HEART DISEASE

Antioxidants, Cholesterol & Heart Disease

CHAPTER 3:

OXIDIZED LDL

DISCOVER

HOW DOES CHOLESTEROL (OR LDL) PRODUCE A BLOCKAGE IN AN ARTERY?

Scientists knew for many years that cholesterol and LDL were involved in producing a plaque in a vessel. As discussed previously, the association between cholesterol and heart disease was so strong that there had to be a cause-and-effect relationship between the two. However, it has been very difficult to define in a biochemical manner precisely how

---

Antioxidants, Cholesterol & Heart Disease

cholesterol initiates plaque generation. From a scientific stand point, one must understand the biochemical process of how a plaque forms before one can develop and implement strategies to combat plaque formation.

Two major advances in the last 10-15 years have helped us dramatically in our understanding of the atherogenic process. The most important of the two was the research which allowed us to understand the pathways involved in LDL transport into tissue. The discovery of specific LDL receptors on cells which regulated the entry of cholesterol and LDL from the blood into the cell was a major breakthrough. This then allowed us to take this knowledge and apply it to disorders in cholesterol metabolism which were strongly associated with heart disease. The most dramatic example of this exists in a special population of people who have abnormally high cholesterol levels. Their circulating LDL and cholesterol levels are almost 10 times as high as normal people. These individuals also suffer from premature heart attacks with many not surviving past 20-30 years old. It was discovered that these individuals have a genetic defect which results in the absence of receptors for LDL in the cells of their body. Because there are no receptors for LDL on the cell surface, LDL cannot enter the cells efficiently and the LDL levels build up in the blood. There's no where for the LDL to go except to form fatty streaks and then fatty plaques in the vessels in which the LDL is in constant contact. The atherogenic process becomes exaggerated and accelerated so much so that the patients exhibit symptoms of heart disease decades before the normal, healthy individual. This work, therefore, accentuates the importance of the LDL receptor in clearing LDL cholesterol from the blood. Obviously then, any substances which influence the number of LDL receptors will affect the LDL concentration in the blood and, therefore, ultimately alter the rate of the atherogenic process which is occurring in the arteries. More information on such substances will be discussed later in the book (see Chapter 5).

The second major advance in our understanding of how the atherogenic process occurs in arteries is very current and still on-going. Research on this aspect of atherosclerosis research is now progressing at a very rapid pace largely because of the potential importance of the information to be generated from the work. The research involves understanding how LDL and cholesterol actually create a plaque. From the research discussed above on LDL receptors, we have learnt that receptors regulate the concentration of LDL in the blood. This strengthened our knowledge of why high levels of LDL in the blood are so well correlated with plaque formation in the artery and heart disease. However, it did not tell us the precise biochemical mechanism for how and why these high circulating LDL molecules begin to build up a plaque in the arterial wall. The answer appears to reside in a modification of the LDL. Research has recently demonstrated that LDL must be oxidatively modified before it becomes a truly dangerous atherogenic agent. Once oxidized, the LDL is capable of transforming various cells in the arterial wall into fat laden cells called "foam cells" which dominate in an atherosclerotic plaque. Normal, unmodified LDL cannot accomplish this transformation. Oxidized LDL has its own special receptor on the cell surface which is very different structurally and functionally than the conventional LDL receptor. Oxidized LDL is carried into cells of the arterial wall at a far faster rate than normal LDL and its entry appears to be uncontrolled. No matter how much oxidized LDL comes into the cells of the arterial wall, the host cell cannot appear to stop its entry by altering the expression of the oxidized LDL receptor on the cell's surface. The end result is that the cholesterol continues to enter the cell, eventually it becomes transformed into one big, fatty, foam cell and the process is repeated over and over on countless cells until the plaque containing these foam cells grows larger and larger.

Antioxidants, Cholesterol & Heart Disease

HOW DOES LDL BECOME OXIDIZED?

For the most part, we do not ingest oxidized cholesterol from our foods. Oxidized fats are primarily produced within our body. However, there are exceptions. For example, the East Indian food ghee contains large amounts of oxidized cholesterol. Ghee is actually a type of butter which has been cooked over and over again. In the process of cooking the butter repeatedly, the cholesterol and fats within the butter become oxidized. Ghee is eaten primarily during religious rites by Hindus. Whether enough ghee is eaten to be harmful to the health or whether ingestion of ghee is harmful at all is currently unclear. In any case, for the majority of people, the ingestion of oxidized fats with their food is not a matter of concern. Once cholesterol is taken into the body it is carried in the blood in the form of LDL. LDL also does not appear to be oxidized to any significant degree as it circulates through the blood. Instead, the LDL appears to be oxidized primarily as it is transported from the blood stream to the cells that require it. As it comes in contact with cells in the arterial wall itself or just under it, the cells release substances which oxidize the LDL. Just about every type of cell in this locale has been shown to have the capacity to oxidize LDL: fibroblasts, endothelial cells, smooth muscle cells, and macrophages to name a few, but the cell names are really unimportant for our purposes. How they accomplish the oxidation is important.

Most cells in the body produce substances called "oxygen-derived free radicals" as a normal, regular event during the use of oxygen by the cell for energy. These "free radicals", as they are usually shortened to, are largely unstable, highly reactive molecules which are quickly inactivated by the cell in various manners. Normally then, free radicals are not a threat to our body at all. However, for reasons which are not altogether clear as yet, conditions exist where the concentration of free radicals in the cell increases. This increase is either due to an unusual over-production of the free radicals or due to a malfunction in the systems which normally inactivate the free radicals. In either case, the end result is that these highly reactive free radicals are now available for action and diffuse out into the space surrounding the cells to attack all and anything within hailing distance. Free radicals will oxidize proteins and fats. Fats are particularly susceptible to oxidation. Since LDL is essentially one big ball of fat, it is a prime target for free radicals to oxidize. Picture it: the free radical stealthily slip slides on out of the cell to launch a sneak attack upon the most unsuspecting LDL that it can find! Yum! Yum! An easy meal which offers little resistance. The oxidized LDL is now primed for its own attack upon some of the very cells which oxidized it. After all, fair's fair. You change my composition and I'll change yours! The oxidized LDL will now enter cells like macrophages and smooth muscle cells in the arterial wall to transform them into the fat laden foam cells which will begin the process of plaque formation.

Antioxidants, Cholesterol & Heart Disease

CHAPTER 4:

ANTIOXIDANTS AND LDL

HOW IS THE OXIDATION OF LDL STOPPED?

Since most cells produce free radicals during the course of their normal function, and knowing that these free radicals are very reactive and dangerous, it is only

Antioxidants, Cholesterol & Heart Disease

logical for us to assume that these very same cells must contain some mechanism to inactivate the free radicals very efficiently or all of the cells would be dead quite quickly. Fortunately, they do. Scavenger systems, as they are called, rapidly inactivate the free radicals to harmless substances (like water in some cases). These free radical scavengers are primarily located within the cell. This is probably the ideal place for them. It insures that the free radicals are inactivated at the source of their production before they can begin to wield their oxidative axe and create any cellular damage. However, if the free radicals are not inactivated and do manage to sneak out of the cell, LDL itself contains several defence mechanisms. Within LDL are several compounds which are fats themselves (or associate well with fatty molecules) and function to inactivate free radicals. These compounds are collectively referred to as "antioxidants" because of their capacity to resist the oxidation process. The most important of these antioxidants is alpha-tocopherol, more commonly known as Vitamin E. Vitamin E hitches a ride with LDL as it courses through the arteries and veins of your body. It is a very efficient antioxidant which can prevent free radicals from oxidizing LDL. Another antioxidant which is found within LDL is beta-carotene (an ingredient of, yes, you guessed it -

carrots!). Both of these compounds along with others provide the LDL with its very own front line of defence against the rampaging hordes of free radicals which may attempt to rape and pillage its virgin fat contents.

Other antioxidants have also been identified which are not associated with LDL. Lately, it seems like new antioxidants are being discovered almost every day and the list is growing rapidly. Many of the compounds we already knew, it's just that we didn't realize their antioxidative capacities. The potency of the various antioxidants varies, some are extremely efficient free radical inactivators, some are less active. Some of the antioxidants, like Vitamin E are found in many places: on LDL, on the cell surface, within the cell, etc. Vitamin E is clearly one of the best antioxidants.

WHY IS LDL OXIDIZED IF WE HAVE ALL THESE ANTIOXIDANTS IN OUR BODY?

As described previously, sometimes the production of free radicals is so great that it overwhelms our antioxidant protection systems. The reasons for this are unclear. Other times the endogenous antioxidant systems are defective. This could be because they are not working properly or, more likely, they are not present in the body in sufficient quantities to defend in an adequate manner against the free radical challenge. Preliminary data has suggested that LDL isolated from patients with documented coronary artery disease (clinically significant blockages in the arteries supplying the heart) was very different from the LDL isolated from healthy, asymptomatic individuals. The difference appeared to be in the ability of the LDL to resist oxidation by a free radical generating system. The LDL from the heart disease patients was more easily oxidized than the LDL from healthy subjects. This would suggest that the endogenous protection mechanisms against free radical induced oxidation were deficient in the LDL taken from the heart disease patients. Deficiencies in Vitamin E are a potential source of the problem, but this was not tested. Interestingly, a similar result was found with people who smoke cigarettes. LDL taken from smokers was more easily oxidized by free radicals than LDL taken from non-smokers. Again, the results suggested that the LDL antioxidant mechanisms may be deficient in smokers. If LDL from smokers is less resistant to free radical attack, this would leave smokers more susceptible to the development of atherosclerosis and heart disease. Ultimately, this may explain why cigarette smoking is an important risk factor for heart disease. Maintenance of the antioxidant defence mechanisms in our body, therefore, should represent an important strategy to guard against the attack of heart disease.

Antioxidants, Cholesterol & Heart Disease

IS IT ONLY LDL WHICH IS OXIDIZED?

Do you remember HDL ("good" cholesterol; Chapter 1)?   HDL has the opposite job of LDL. HDL was responsible for taking the cholesterol away from the tissue and helping in the process of ridding the body of cholesterol.

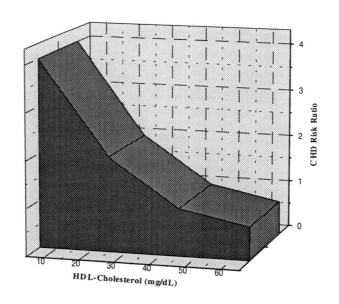

Recent scientific studies have shown that HDL is also susceptible to being oxidized by free radicals. This oxidation of HDL changes the function of HDL dramatically. Once oxidized, HDL becomes far less effective in removing cholesterol from the cells. Altogether then, the oxidation of HDL and LDL by free radicals is a double-whammy to the body. First (Pow!): oxidation of LDL makes cholesterol deposition and plaque formation easier. Second (Wham!): oxidation of HDL makes the reversal of this process more difficult. The end result is bad news for you and me.

CAN ANYTHING BE DONE TO INCREASE THE ANTIOXIDANT DEFENCES IN OUR BODY?

Another way of phrasing this question might be: Would supplementation of the diet with antioxidants (like, for example, vitamin E) be beneficial to ward off the effects of free radicals and retard the atherosclerotic process in your heart? Currently, it is believed that such supplementation could be beneficial but the scientific data are still not complete on this important question. Scientific research has shown that drugs like probucol which are designed to reduce the oxidative effects of free radicals on substances like LDL are very effective in retarding plaque formation in arteries of animals. Vitamin E supplements given to primates fed a high cholesterol diet reduced the symptoms of atherosclerosis. In other studies, animals chronically deficient in Vitamins E and C exhibit accelerated development of atherosclerotic lesions.

Because of these and other encouraging results, clinical trials on large numbers of people are currently underway to more effectively evaluate the benefit of drugs or vitamins which act as antioxidants.

Two studies recently published in the New England Journal of Medicine in 1993 represent the only extensive investigations of the influence of vitamin E on heart disease. Examining nearly 40,000 men aged 40-75 years old over a four year period, the investigators found that higher intakes of vitamin E were associated with a significantly lower risk of heart disease. Carotene intake also appeared to protect against heart disease in those who smoke or previously smoked. In another study of some 87,000 women aged 34-59 years old, scientists found that vitamin E supplementation reduced the risk of heart disease if taken continuously for more than two years. Short periods of vitamin E supplementation did not appear to help the women. The two studies suggest that vitamin E may help reduce the risk of atherosclerotic disease in both men and women. Preliminary studies from Europe have revealed death from heart disease was reduced if blood vitamin E levels were high. Low vitamin E levels also have been associated with the early appearance of angina (chest pains). The results overall suggest but do not yet conclusively prove that supplementation of the diet with antioxidants will lower the risk of heart disease. Further large scale clinical trials are needed to confirm the works published in the New England Journal of Medicine.

Antioxidants, Cholesterol & Heart Disease

How much vitamin E should you ingest? It is impossible to answer this with any certainty in the abscence of more studies on the effects of vitamin E on coronary heart disease. However, men who took at least 100 IU per day for at least two years did significantly reduce their chances of having heart disease. At present, it would be a safe, prudent step to supplement the diet with vitamin E or other antioxidants, or to ingest foods rich in antioxidants. There are no data to suggest that a modest supplementation of such compounds would hurt the body and there appears to be more and more indirect evidence suggesting that it will help. The more evidence that is produced (even if it is indirect) indicating that antioxidant supplementation is beneficial in the fight against heart disease, the stronger the argument becomes that this type of therapy should be more actively encouraged now.

HOW DO I KNOW IF THE ANTIOXIDANT LEVELS IN MY BLOOD ARE ADEQUATE?

The National Cancer Institute and the National Academy of Sciences in the United States recommends that at least two fruits and three vegetables per day is a desirable intake. Fruits and vegetables are rich in antioxidants (see Part III). Recent data indicates that only 9% of Americans actually eat this amount of fruits and vegetables every day. Many European countries are far lower than Americans in their ingestion of fruits and vegetables. Obviously then, the vast majority of the population has a great opportunity to increase their antioxidant levels and improve their health. How do you know if you are ingesting appropriate amounts of antioxidants? Even if you are eating properly, absorption of these antioxidants from the gut varies considerably from patient to patient complicating the matter further. Can antioxidant levels be measured? The answer, fortunately, is affirmative. The Pantox Corporation (4622 Sante Fe Street, San Diego, California 92109) has recently begun to offer a unique service to measure the antioxidant profile of your blood. Serum

Antioxidants, Cholesterol & Heart Disease

samples from your blood can be sent to the Pantox laboratories by your doctor via a dry ice mailing package provided by Pantox. The laboratory will measure cholesterol, LDL, HDL and triglyceride levels in your serum to provide a lipid profile. They will do the same for antioxidants like Vitamins C, E and A and beta carotene. Other testing is available if required. For example, iron levels in your serum, the fatty acid profile (saturated versus unsaturated) and the Coenzyme Q10 levels can also be determined. The patient and their doctor are ultimately provided with an entire antioxidant profile which describes what the patients' relative risk for cardiovascular disease is. This can be done before and after a diet and/or an exercise program is instituted to provide the patient with tangible evidence of how his or her efforts are helping. Many insurance companies and work place health policies are now covering this expense.

CAN I LOWER MY CHOLESTEROL LEVELS WITH VITAMIN E?

Absolutely not. The ingestion of vitamin E is intended as a supplement to the other approaches prescribed by your physician. Careful regulation of your diet, regular exercise and vitamin E supplementation are prudent measures to prevent the occurrence of high blood cholesterol and heart disease. Vitamin E use on its own (without adhering to the other lifestyle modifications) is unlikely to help to any significant degree. If diet and exercise are unsuccessful as first line defences and your cholesterol levels remain elevated, then your doctor will likely prescribe medication to help control the cholesterol levels. Don't be alarmed: this is a normal progression in the treatment of high blood cholesterol.

Antioxidants, Cholesterol & Heart Disease

PART III

PREVENTION: FIGHTING THE GOOD FIGHT AGAINST CHOLESTEROL AND HEART DISEASE

Antioxidants, Cholesterol & Heart Disease

CHAPTER 5:

LOWERING YOUR CHOLESTEROL LEVELS

Cholesterol-free home

> **I HAVE A FRIEND WHO EXERCISED REGULARLY, ATE CAREFULLY, AND STILL DIED FROM A HEART ATTACK. WHY SHOULD I FOLLOW SUCH A LIFE STYLE IF IT DOESN'T WORK?**

Following a healthy life style which includes regular exercise and eating foods low in fat content does not make you totally

Antioxidants, Cholesterol & Heart Disease

immune from heart disease. You still may die from complications incurred during the progression of coronary artery disease. However, a healthy life style will reduce your chances of incurring heart disease. Statistically, in a large population of people, your chances of having a heart attack will be less than they would be if you didn't have a healthy life style. Most importantly, adhering to a healthy life style will slow the progression of coronary artery disease and probably lessen the severity of a heart attack if it does occur. Although it is almost impossible to prove, your friend probably would have succumbed to heart disease and his fatal heart attack a lot sooner in his life if he had not maintained a regular pattern of exercise and a healthy, sensible diet. We cannot prove this but we do know that the atherosclerosis process is accelerated whenever the diet is poor (for example, contains a high percentage of fatty products). The converse, then, is also true: regulate your diet, exercise to reduce obesity, and you will retard or (if you're lucky) prevent the development of artery blockages which will eventually land you in the hospital (or worse).

IF I AM SUCCESSFUL IN LOWERING MY BLOOD CHOLESTEROL, CAN I REVERSE THE HEART DISEASE OR ARE THE BLOCKAGES IN MY ARTERIES PERMANENT?

This is an important question for those already suffering from the complications of coronary artery disease. If you resist all those chocolate eclairs, deny yourself triple scoop ice cream cones (let them not eat cake!) and huff and puff your way back into a shape which no longer gets you mistaken for the Pillsbury doughboy, are you going to get better, or, are you just stopping any further damage from occurring? The answer, fortunately, is encouraging. The blockage or plaque which is in the arteries of your heart can actually regress if you reduce your blood cholesterol levels successfully. In other words, if you have the ability to lower your blood cholesterol levels, the blockage in your coronary artery (which, remember, ultimately caused the chest pain or the heart attack) will not only stop getting larger but, because of your dedicated efforts, will actually begin to get smaller. That's the good news. The bad news is that the process of reversing the plaque from a growing blockage to one which is getting smaller is a very slow process. This only makes sense. It took you many, many years to make that plug in your arteries: the time course for reversing this process must also be extremely slow. However, every little bit helps. A small reduction in blood cholesterol will significantly reduce your chances of incurring another heart attack. It is crucial for the cardiac patient to realize that all the sacrifice and hard work is paying off in a big way: their life is being saved! The regression of the plaque may be frustratingly slow but it's not often that we are fortunate enough to be promised such an important physical "salvation"!

I CAREFULLY CHOOSE FOODS LOW IN CHOLESTEROL BUT I STILL CAN'T SEEM TO LOWER MY BLOOD CHOLESTEROL CONCENTRATION. WHY CAN'T I?

The answer to this common question has several parts to it. First, it is important to recognize that controlling your dietary intake of cholesterol is not the only factor which will influence your blood cholesterol levels. There are actually three factors which will have a major impact upon how high your blood cholesterol levels will rise. These are: 1) the amount of cholesterol that you consume. Obviously, the more food you eat which is high in cholesterol, the higher your blood cholesterol will be; 2) the total amount of calories that you ingest. Even if you eat foods low in cholesterol, if you take in a lot of calories, your blood levels of cholesterol will rise; 3) the amount of saturated fats that you eat. The more foods that you ingest that are high in saturated fat content, the higher your blood cholesterol will rise. Foods like cooking oils, snack foods, hamburgs, hot dogs, luncheon meats, whole milk and cheeses are some of the more common sources of saturated fats in the North American diet. Of course, the

Antioxidants, Cholesterol & Heart Disease

careful shopper can always pick up varieties of even these foods which are now available in the supermarket in a "low-in-saturated-fats" form. Keep an eye out for them the next time you go grocery shopping.

It is important for us to point out here that the health conscious shopper is now an important consumer these days and advertisers target them and attempt to win their business with products that are designed to be low in cholesterol or even cholesterol free. **BEWARE! BE SMART!** Potato chip advertising is a common example of how some products in the grocery store will attempt to manipulate a person's limited knowledge of what they should eat and what they should avoid. Advertisements for many snacks like potato chips claim in big, bold letters on the bag that their product is cholesterol-free. This is true. After all, as we stated earlier in the book, vegetables do not contain cholesterol. Potato chips will not contain cholesterol either if they are cooked in an oil which contains no cholesterol. Thus, the advertisement is absolutely correct: the potato chips are cholesterol-free. However, does this now mean that the cholesterol-

concious dieter can indulge in the crispy little rascals to his heart's content (no pun intended)? The answer to this question is a resounding "No"! The reason is, of course, because the chips are very high in calories and saturated fats. Both of these factors will undoubtedly raise your blood cholesterol

Antioxidants, Cholesterol & Heart Disease

levels. **DON'T BE FOOLED!** Be watchful of manipulative, partially correct but dangerously misleading advertising! Always remember the triple threat that faces your blood cholesterol level: cholesterol in your foods, total calories ingested, and saturated fats in your diet. All three must be diligently regulated and reduced. All (not just one) will ultimately affect your blood cholesterol level and only the ever-watchful, informed individual will win the fight and turn back the tides of cholesterol flooding his blood stream.

The second part of the answer to the original question involves your own individual genetic make-up. As described previously in the text (Chapter 1), cholesterol exists in your blood as part of a protein complex called LDL. The amount of LDL in your blood is determined by how much cholesterol comes into it (by, for example, your diet) and how much is cleared from the blood stream. It's much like pouring water into a glass which has a hole in the bottom. The amount of water in the glass is determined by how fast we are pouring water into the glass and how fast the water can escape from the hole in the bottom. If the hole is small, more water will fill up the glass. Similarly, an important part of determining your blood LDL levels is not only your diet (cholesterol entering the blood) but also the clearance of LDL from the blood (the hole in the glass). LDL leaves the circulation by being taken up into the cells all over the body and, in particular, the liver. This is regulated by the number of LDL receptors on the cell surfaces (see Chapter 2 for more detail). If the number of receptors is low, LDL cannot be taken up from the blood and cholesterol levels will remain elevated. A number of factors will affect the number of receptors on the cell. One of these factors is genetic. Some people appear to be born with more LDL receptors, others with less. Those who are "receptor-poor" can try to control the cholesterol in their diet all they want and they will still tend to have higher than normal blood LDL (or cholesterol) concentrations.

Antioxidants, Cholesterol & Heart Disease

CHAPTER 6:

OTHER IMPORTANT STRATEGIES TO REGULATE CHOLESTEROL

ARE THERE ANY DRUGS AVAILABLE WHICH WILL LOWER MY BLOOD CHOLESTEROL CONCENTRATION? HOW DO THEY WORK AND ARE THERE ANY SIDE-EFFECTS?

Drug therapy is recommended in three general categories of patients in order to lower the blood cholesterol levels. Patients with extremely high blood cholesterol levels, or patients with mildly elevated blood cholesterol concentration but are at high risk for heart disease from other causes, or patients who have elevated cholesterol levels and are not responding to dietary interventions are all good candidates for drug therapy of one kind or another.

There are several different types of cholesterol-lowering drugs available which work via different mechanisms. Cholesterol is converted into bile acids in the liver. The bile acids normally circulate from the liver into the intestine and back again to the liver. Cholesterol-lowering agents like cholestyramine (Questran) and colestipol (Colestid) bind bile acids in the intestinal area and increase their elimination from the body. The end result is that more cholesterol is excreted and blood cholesterol levels will begin to be lowered. The side-effects of these drugs include constipation, gas and bloating. Usually, the side-effects are not serious.

Another type of cholesterol lowering agent is niacin (nicotinic acid). At normal or low dosages, this drug has no effect on cholesterol levels in the blood. However, at extremely high dosage levels, niacin will significantly lower blood cholesterol levels by inhibiting the liver's ability to produce circulating fats. The precise mechanism whereby it has its effects on the liver are not clear. Side-effects from niacin administration can be extensive. Most patients will immediately show signs of reddening or flushing in the face which can be very irritating. Other patients can have stomach irritations, liver problems and irregular heart beats. Diabetic patients are also susceptible to the side-effects of niacin on sugar tolerance and blood sugar levels.

Drugs like pravastatin (Pravachol), lovastatin (Mevacor) and mevastatin are all very common drugs used in the control of circulating cholesterol concentrations. These drugs work by lowering the capacity of the cell to make its own cholesterol. Furthermore, by having this action, the drugs also indirectly stimulate the capacity of the cell to produce more receptors for LDL on the cell surface. This increased number of LDL receptors on the cells enhances their ability to clear LDL (and thus, cholesterol) from the blood stream. This effect, combined with the inhibition of cholesterol synthesis in the cells, contributes to an overall lowering of the cholesterol and LDL levels in the blood. Generally, these drugs have been well tolerated. The use of these drugs has been recommended in patients with extremely high levels of blood cholesterol and in patients who may have moderately high cholesterol levels but have other complicating risk factors present (for example, diabetes, chest pain, cigarette smoking).

Another class of lipid lowering agents are the fibric acid drugs. These include gemfibrozil (Lopid), clofibrate (Atromid-S or Novo-Fibrate) and fenofibrate (Lipidil) to name just a few. They lower most fat levels in the blood and some can increase the circulating levels of "good" cholesterol as well (HDL). Gemfibrozil has demonstrated a significant effect in reducing coronary heart disease in several large studies. Patients who are being administered the drugs may complain of muscle soreness, irritations in the gastrointestinal area and could experience cholesterol gallstones. Patients with high blood fat levels (not necessarily high cholesterol levles alone) and low HDL levels are candidates for therapy with the fibric acid drugs.

Probucol (Lorelco) is the only drug available today which has been approved for use by the Food and Drug Administration in the United States which has significant antioxidant effects. Actually, probucol has two effects on serum cholesterol. First, it has a cholesterol lowering effect of its own. Its mechanism of action is not entirely clear. Second, probucol can inhibit the oxidation of LDL. It is significant to note that in controlled studies of probucol's actions, when the cholesterol lowering ability of probucol and another drug were equalized, probucol reduced the severity of atherosclerotic plaque development in arteries to a greater extent than the other agent. This is important because it emphasizes the significance of probucol's antioxidative capacity. It suggests that a drug which possesses antioxidant capabilities will have a better protective effect against heart disease than one which does not (if all other factors are equal). Probucol, unfortunately, is not the perfect drug. It is not as strong in its antioxidative abilities as would be desired. It also produces some changes in the electrical characteristics of the heart, may reduce the levels of "good" cholesterol (HDL), and can produce diarrhea, some stomach irritations and sickness. Clearly, there is a greater need for more research on antioxidant drugs and developing more compounds which contain antioxidant potential. Probucol is best suited to patients with mildly elevated serum cholesterol levels.

At present, probucol is not a "front-line", first step drug used in the treatment of high blood cholesterol levels. The usual progression for the treatment of an alarmingly high cholesterol concentration in the blood is first to impose dietary restrictions and counseling. If this is unsuccessful or the results are less than desirable, then active pharmacological therapy can be recommended. A bile binding agent like cholestyramine is commonly employed as the primary drug of choice by most physicians in the treatment of moderate to severe blood cholesterol levels. If the results are still not acceptable, then combining one type of cholesterol lowering agent with another one which works via a different mechanism is often employed. Another alternative is simply to change the drug entirely (especially if the drug is poorly tolerated by the patient) and try another agent which again has a different mechanism of lowering the blood cholesterol concentration.

WHAT ARE POLYUNSATURATED FATS AND WHY ARE THEY GOOD FOR US?

Cholesterol is not the only type of fat found in the body and in the foods that we ingest. Another common type of fat is called a fatty acid because of its chemical properties and composition. Dietary fats contain several different sub-categories of fatty acids. These fatty acids can be saturated, monounsaturated or polyunsaturated. The differences amongst these fatty acids refers to the number of hydrogen atoms which are associated with the carbon chain which is the backbone of the fatty acid moiety. A saturated fatty acid contains a full contingent of hydrogen with it. A monounsaurated fatty acid has one space left which is not being filled by a hydrogen atom. A polyunsaturated fatty acid has more than one space free for hydrogen atoms to bind to it. It's much like seats on a bus. A saturated fatty acid has all of its seats full. There's no more room on the bus. A monounsaturated fatty acid has only one seat empty and the polyunsaturated fatty acid bus has a number of empty seats.

SATURATED FATS
BUS

The study of fatty acids is worthy of our discussion because these molecules appear to have important effects on cholesterol levels in the blood and heart disease. In this case, the bad guys are the saturated fats. The good guys are the mono- and polyunsaturated fats. Let's deal with the bad saturated fats first. Animal fats are typically rich in saturated fats. Vegetable oils will also contain saturated fatty acids. The tropical vegetable oils like coconut oil, palm oil, and cocoa butter are particularly rich in saturated fat content. Our dietary intake of saturated fats is almost equally divided three ways amongst meats, dairy products and snacking foods and oils. The higher the intake of saturated fats is, the higher the likelihood that blood cholesterol levels will rise. Of course, the higher cholesterol concentration spells danger and the chance of significant heart disease increases too. The mechanism whereby saturated fats

Antioxidants, Cholesterol & Heart Disease

increase blood cholesterol concentrations is not altogether clear. However, it appears that saturated fats in the diet have the capacity to inhibit the activity or expression of LDL receptors on the surface of cells in the body. Without LDL receptors on the cell surface to take up the circulating LDL in the blood stream, LDL levels build up in the blood. This, of course, has important implications for the development of clinical complications associated with heart disease.

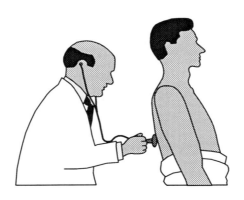

IF I INCREASE THE FIBER CONTENT OF MY DIET, WILL IT REDUCE MY CHANCES OF HAVING A HEART ATTACK?

Yes and no. There are two general types of fibers which are found in the food that we eat. One is called soluble fiber, the other is insoluble fiber. Both of these types of fiber are not digestible. They remain in the gastro-intestinal tract and aid in colon function. Insoluble fiber is the kind of fiber with which most people are familiar. The most common form is cellulose which is found in foods like wheat bran and adds bulk to our stools. It appears to have no influence on blood cholesterol or LDL levels. Soluble fibers include some gums and pectins. One particular kind of gum is found commonly in beans and oat bran. Soluble fibers do appear to have a cholesterol-lowering effect (approximately 5-10% decrease). However, ingestion of large amounts of soluble fiber normally leads to gastro-intestinal discomfort such that most people discontinue their use. Therefore, ingestion of fiber may help to prevent your death from cancer of the colon and heart disease. However, from a practical viewpoint, although *you* may not die, the gas

Antioxidants, Cholesterol & Heart Disease

‖you produce may kill all of your friends (Just‖
‖kidding!).‖

IS EXERCISE IMPORTANT?

Exercise is very important for a number of reasons. It is recommended that one follow an exercise program for at least three times per week. Each exercise period should last for a duration of at least 15 minutes. The cardiovascular benefits of exercise include the following :

- ♥ May lower blood pressure in people who have hypertension.
- ♥ May increase your HDL (good cholesterol) level.
- ♥ May lower total serum cholesterol level.
- ♥ May lower LDL cholesterol level.
- ♥ May decrease your resting heart rate.
- ♥ May decrease your triglyceride level.
- ♥ May help to lower blood sugar levels in diabetics.
- ♥ Helps in weight control.
- ♥ May help in stress reduction.
- ♥ May help to increase endogenous antioxidant levels.

Apart from the cardiovascular benefits, exercise also helps by reducing fatigue, tension, and anxiety. Exercise also may improve physical appearance and give the exerciser a sense of well-being and confidence.

CHAPTER 7:

NUTRITIONAL ADVICE

ARE THERE ANY GENERAL NUTRITIONAL GUIDELINES WHICH I SHOULD FOLLOW?

To maintain a healthy heart, it is important to consider the following six dietary objectives:

1.   reduce cholesterol intake
2.   reduce fat intake
3.   reduce caloric intake

Antioxidants, Cholesterol & Heart Disease

4. increase the intake of antioxidants, vitamins and minerals
5. increase intake of complex carbohydrates
6. increase intake of dietary fiber.

WHAT FOODS SHOULD I EAT WHICH ARE LOW IN CHOLESTEROL?

Dietary cholesterol is found mainly in egg yolks, certain shellfish, organ meats, and to a lesser extent other meats and dairy products.

MAJOR SOURCES OF DIETARY CHOLESTEROL

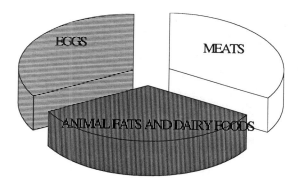

Cholesterol intake should not exceed 250 mg/day. To compare the cholesterol content of some common foods, consider the following information.

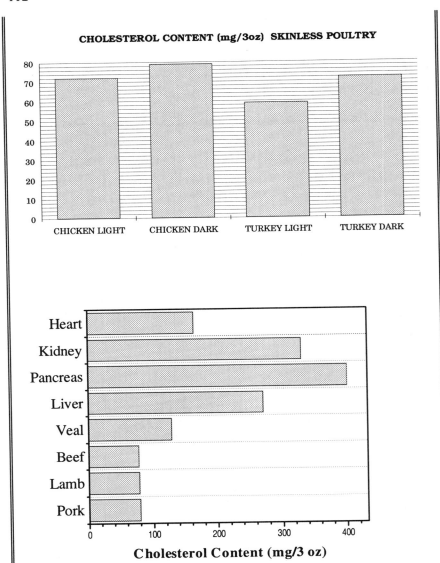

CHOLESTEROL CONTENT (mg/3oz) SKINLESS POULTRY

Cholesterol Content (mg/3 oz)

Antioxidants, Cholesterol & Heart Disease

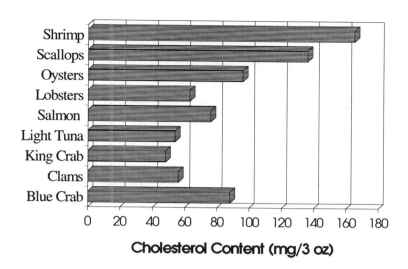

Cholesterol Content (mg/3 oz)

The intake of fat and cholesterol can be reduced by substituting poultry without skin, lean meats, and fish instead of fatty meats. Further, one may consume low-fat  dairy products instead of those with a high fat content. It is also recommended that one consume considerably higher quantities of fruits and vegetables, cereals and legumes while restricting the amount of oils, egg yolks, fried and other fatty meats. (See later in this Chapter for details about the cholesterol content of foods).

Antioxidants, Cholesterol & Heart Disease

CONSIDERATIONS IN CHOOSING A
CHOLESTEROL LOWERING DIET

FRUITS
VEGETABLES
LEGUMES
WHOLE-GRAIN BREADS
CEREALS
OTHER GRAINS
SEEDS AND NUTS
POULTRY
FISH
SHELLFISH
LOW-FAT DAIRY PRODUCTS
EGG WHITES
VEGETABLE OILS THAT ARE HIGH IN UNSATURATED FATS

There are a number of suggestions that are recommended for anyone wishing to lower their cholesterol by diet. Generally, the overall plan should be a nutritionally balanced cholesterol-lowering diet. Listed below are recommendations of the various nutrients and their respective percentage of total calories.

NUTRIENTS	RECOMMENDATIONS (% OF TOTAL CALORIES)
CARBOHYDRATES	BETWEEN 50% TO 60%
PROTEINS	15%
TOTAL FATS	LESS THAN 30%
SATURATED	LESS THAN 7%
MONOUNSATURATED	BETWEEN 10% TO 15%
POLYUNSATURATED	LESS THAN 10%

Note that total calories means amount of calories needed to achieve desirable weight (see following pages for information about calories and body weight).

Antioxidants, Cholesterol & Heart Disease

HOW DO I REDUCE MY FAT INTAKE?

The fat content of foods is measured in grams. The average woman with elevated cholesterol, for example, should limit her fat intake to 53 grams or less per day (men, 75 grams or less per day). By knowing what the upper limit of their daily fat intake is, individuals then can use the information on the content of foods to make judgements on how suitable a particular food is for a lower fat diet. Overall, it is recommended that the total intake of fat does not exceed 30% percent of total daily calories, while saturated fatty acids, often found in animal products, should be less than 10% of calories. Saturated fats are linked to elevation of LDL cholesterol. By consuming excessive quantities of foods that are rich in calories, cholesterol, and saturated fats, individuals run the risk of further increasing their already elevated serum cholesterol levels. Studies have estimated that for every 100 mg of cholesterol increase per 1000 calories/day, the serum cholesterol will raise by approximately 8-10 mg/dl.

WHAT ARE THE FOOD CHOICES FOR REDUCING SATURATED FATS AND CHOLESTEROL?

RECOMMENDED CHOICES

POULTRY, MEATS AND FISH
FISH

SHELLFISH

POULTRY(SKINLESS)

LEAN BEEF,LAMB,PORK

VEAL

DAIRY PRODUCTS
SKIM MILK OR LOW-FAT

LOW FAT YOGURT

LOW FAT COTTAGE CHEESE

LOW FAT CHEESE

SHERBERT

BREADS AND CEREALS
BAKED GOODS USING UNSATURATED OILS

LOW FAT CRACKERS

RICE

PASTA

WHOLE GRAIN BREADS AND CEREALS

EGGS
EGG WHITES

MODERATE CONSUMPTION

Antioxidants, Cholesterol & Heart Disease

FRUITS AND VEGETABLES
FRUITS

VEGETABLES

FATS AND OILS
UNSATURATED VEGETABLEOILS

SALAD DRESSING FROM VEGETABLE OILS

SEEDS AND NUTS

Although meats are generally thought to contain large amounts of fat, this is not necessarily the case. Different meat types can vary considerably in their fat content. Generally, organ meats are rather low in fat. However the same meats are high in cholesterol (be careful!).

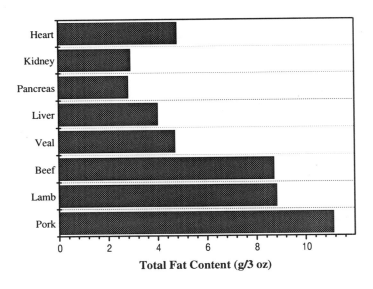

Total Fat Content (g/3 oz)

Antioxidants, Cholesterol & Heart Disease

The fat content of fish varies considerable depending on the type of fish. Generally, all fish and seafood products are low in fat with the exception of salmon and oysters.

TOTAL FAT CONTENT (g/3 oz) OF SKINLESS POULTRY

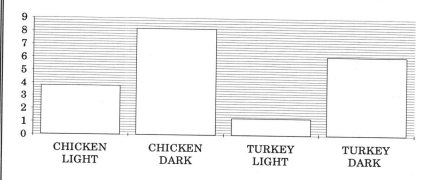

The colour of the meat is also a significant factor to consider when one is concerned about their fat intake. Light meats have approximately half the fat content of their dark meat counterparts.

Antioxidants, Cholesterol & Heart Disease

WHAT FOODS CONTAIN MONO- AND POLYUNSATURATED FATTY ACIDS?

As previously mentioned, particular fatty acids have different effects on health. Saturated fatty acids and dietary cholesterol tend to increase serum cholesterol levels, thereby increasing the risk of cardiovascular disease. For example, palmitic, lauric and myristic acids have the greatest cholesterol raising effect. Sources of these fatty acids include dairy and meat products and some vegetable oils (coconut, palm).

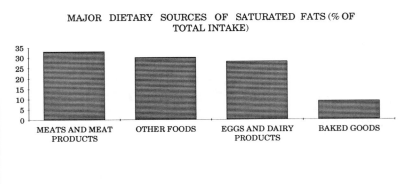

MAJOR DIETARY SOURCES OF SATURATED FATS (% OF TOTAL INTAKE)

It is recommended that one chooses oils that are rich in monounsaturated fatty acids.

SOURCES OF MONOUNSATURATED FATTY ACIDS

OLIVE OIL
FLAX SEED OIL
CANOLA OIL
SAFFLOWER OIL
SUNFLOWER OIL
SOYBEAN OIL
AVACADO OIL
PECAN OIL
HAZELNUT OIL
PEANUT OIL

Polyunsaturated fatty acids are another type that are recommended. There are two types of polyunsaturated fatty acids, omega-6 and omega-3; both are essential nutrients and are not synthesized by the body. Omega-6 polyunsaturated fatty acids are found in various plant oils, including safflower, sunflower, soyabean and corn oils. Omega-3 polyunsaturated fatty acids are found in marine fish like mackerel and salmon and some plant oils.

SOURCES OF POLYUNSATURATED FATTY ACIDS

FLAX SEED OIL
SAFFLOWER OIL
SUNFLOWER OIL
SOYBEAN OIL
CORN OIL

Antioxidants, Cholesterol & Heart Disease

HOW DO I REDUCE MY CALORIC INTAKE?

Excess weight is associated with an increased risk for cardiovascular disease. The risks seem to decline following a prolonged reduction in weight. Obesity in itself may not be a predisposition to the development of coronary heart disease. Rather, obesity promotes the presence of other risk factors such as high cholesterol, high blood pressure, and diabetes which consequently will increase your chances of heart disease. Increased abdominal fat seems to be a higher risk factor than fat deposits in the hips and thighs. Foods that are high in fat and high in sugar (e.g. desserts, baked goods) are the primary culprits for high calories. Furthermore, foods high in sugar content represent empty calories with little nutritive value.

HEIGHT-WEIGHT TABLE

HEIGHT	AGES 19-34	AGES 35 AND OLDER
5'0"	97-128 lbs	108-138 lbs
5'1"	101-132 lbs	111-143 lbs
5'2"	104-137 lbs	115-148 lbs
5'3"	107-141 lbs	119-152 lbs
5'4"	111-146 lbs	122-157 lbs
5'5"	114-150 lbs	126-162 lbs
5'6"	118-155 lbs	130-167 lbs
5'7"	121-160 lbs	134-172 lbs
5'8"	125-164 lbs	138-178 lbs
5'9"	129-169 lbs	142-183 lbs
5'10"	132-174 lbs	146-188 lbs
5'11"	136-179 lbs	151-194 lbs
6'0"	140-184 lbs	155-199 lbs
6'1"	144-189 lbs	159-205 lbs
6'2"	148-195 lbs	164-210 lbs
6'3"	152-200 lbs	168-216 lbs
6'4"	156-205 lbs	173-222 lbs
6'5"	160-211 lbs	177-228 lbs
6'6"	164-216 lbs	182-234 lbs

This table lists average weight for your height and age. For each range listed, higher weights generally apply to men and lower weights for women. Please note, this table does not take into consideration factors such as medical problems, fat distribution or content.

Antioxidants, Cholesterol & Heart Disease

CALORIC CONTENT OF VARIOUS FOODS

BEVERAGES	Calories	Cholesterol	Fat
		(milligrams)	(grams)
Soft Drinks (12 oz)	155	0	0
Soft Drinks (12 oz) Diet	1	0	0
Seltzer	0	0	0
Milk (Whole) (8 oz)	160	35	9
Milk (Skim) (8 oz)	85	4	trace
Buttermilk (8 oz)	100	9	2
Lemonade (sweetened) (8 oz)	100	0	0
Kool Aid (8 oz)	100	0	0
Tomato Juice (8 oz)	4	0	0
Orange Juice (8 oz)	120	0	0
Grape Juice (8 oz)	160	0	0
Cranberry Juice (8 oz)	143	0	0
Apple Juice (8 oz)	120	0	0
Gatorade (8 oz)	50	0	0
Eggnog (8 oz)	342	149	19
Coffee (1 tbsp cream, 2 tsp sugar)	50	6	2
Cocoa (milk and water, 8 oz)	60	2	3
Cocoa (whole milk, 8 oz)	220	37	9

BREAKFAST FOODS	Calories	Cholesterol	Fat
		(milligrams)	(grams)
Waffles, without syrup, 2	420	120	16
Toast with Butter (1 tbsp), 1	170	35	13
Pancakes (without syrup), 2	120	32	4
Oatmeal, 1 cup	130	0	2
French Toast (w/o syrup), 2	300	224	14
English Muffin, 1	140	0	1
Boiled/Poached Eggs, 2	140	426	12
Scrambled Eggs, 2	180	426	14
Donut	210	20	12
Danish	275	49	12

Antioxidants, Cholesterol & Heart Disease

Croissant	300	15	12
Rice Crispies, 1 cup	110	0	0
Raisin Bran, 1 cup	160	0	trace
Frosted Flakes, 1 cup	165	0	1
Captain Crunch, 1 cup	161	0	3
Corn Flakes, 1 cup	110	0	trace
Cheerios, 1 cup	88	0	1
Bran Muffin	140	28	6
Blueberry Muffin	135	19	5
Bagel with cream cheese	300	30	10
Bagel, plain	200	0	0

DAIRY PRODUCTS	**Calories**	**Cholesterol**	**Fat**
		(milligrams)	(grams)
Yogurt (flavoured, low fat)	230	10	6
Sour Cream, 2 tbsp	50	10	6
Mayonnaise, 1 tbsp	100	8	11
Margarine, 1 tbsp	100	0	12
Ice Cream, 4 oz	175	12	12
Frozen Yogurt, 4 oz	80	0	0
Cheese (Cottage, 2%), 1/2 c	80	0	trace
Cheese, 1 oz	105	30	9
Butter, 1 tbsp	100	33	12

DESSERTS	**Calories**	**Cholesterol**	**Fat**
		(milligrams)	(grams)
Sundae, Hot Fudge, 1 med	357	27	13
Sundae, Banana Split	615	85	31
Pudding, dietic, non-fat milk	60	1	0
Pudding, flavored, 1/2 c	140	1	4
Pie, Peach, 1 piece	405	0	17
Pie, Lemon Meringue,	355	143	14
Pie, Custard, 1 piece	330	17	17
Pie, Bluebery, 1 piece	380	4	17
Pie, Apple, 1 piece	405	0	18
Jello, 1/2 cup	80	0	0
Cupcake with icing, 1	130	1	5

Antioxidants, Cholesterol & Heart Disease

Cookies, Choc Chip, 4	180	5	9
Cheesecake, 2" piece	280	170	14
Chocolate Cake, 2" piece	250	3	11
Angel Food Cake, 2" piece	110	0	trace

FISH AND POULTRY	Calories	Cholesterol	Fat
		(milligrams)	(grams)
Turkey, white meat, 4 oz	180	69	2
Tuna, canned, waterpack	110	35	trace
Trout, 4 oz	170	82	5
Shrimp, 6 large	45	65	trace
Oysters (raw), 6	58	45	2
Lobster Meat, 4 oz w lemon	110	81	1
Fish Sticks, 5	200	87	12
Crabmeat, imitation, 4 oz	130	53	1
Crabmeat, canned, 3 oz	85	76	1
Chicken Patty, breaded, 3oz	100	26	16
Fried Chicken, 1/2 breast	280	100	18
Fried Chicken, 1 drumstick	120	44	11
Roasted Chicken, 4 oz	200	97	4
Bass, 4 oz	150	87	4

FRUITS	Calories	Cholesterol	Fat
		(milligrams)	(grams)
Watermelon, 1 cup	50	0	0
Strawberries, 1 cup	45	0	0
Raspberries, 1 cup	60	0	0
Plums, 2	70	0	0
Pineapple, fresh, 1 cup	75	0	0
Pear (heavy syrup), 1 cup	188	0	0
Peach, fresh, 1	35	0	0
Orange, 1	65	0	0
Grapes, 1 cup	60	0	0
Grapefruit, 1/2 cup	40	0	0
Cherries, fresh, 10	50	0	0
Cantaloupe, 1/2 cup	60	0	0
Blueberries, fresh, 1/2 cup	40	0	0

Antioxidants, Cholesterol & Heart Disease

Banana, 1	105	0	0
Apricot, 1	16	0	0
Apple, 1	80	0	0

POTATOES	Calories	Cholesterol	Fat
		(milligrams)	(grams)
Mashed potatoes, 1 cup	240	15	12
Fried potatoes, 1 cup	340	0	19
Boiled potato	10	0	0
Baked potato, plain	100	0	0
French Fries, 10 pieces	220	14	13

RED MEAT	Calories	Cholesterol	Fat
		(milligrams)	(grams)
Veal, loin, 3 oz	236	103	8
Porterhouse steak	341	95	12
Top Round steak	218	96	7
Spare Ribs, 4 oz	435	97	37
Pork Sausage, 1 link	265	46	21
Pork Chop, 4 oz	400	110	33
Fried Liver, 4 oz	250	445	9
Hamburger, broiled, lean	185	104	21
Cured Ham, 4 oz	230	65	12
Corned Beef, 4 oz	285	112	21

SALADS	Calories	Cholesterol	Fat
		(milligrams)	(grams)
Tossed, Green, plain	50	0	0
Taco Salad, 1 med	430	15	28
Potato Salad, 1 cup	280	175	18
Pasta Salad, 1 cup	394	48	22
Chicken Salad, 1 cup	360	25	18
Chef Salad, 1 med	309	172	19

Antioxidants, Cholesterol & Heart Disease

SANDWICHES	Calories	Cholesterol (milligrams)	Fat (grams)
Turkey with Gravy	200	32	15
Tuna	280	36	14
Peanut Butter and Jelly	330	0	15
Pastrami	415	68	29
Ham and Cheese	495	89	31
Grilled Cheese	450	70	31
Egg Salad, Open	200	190	16
Club	395	50	26
Chicken Salad	315	63	18
Bologna	360	42	23
Bacon and Tomato, Open	290	22	18

SNACKS	Calories	Cholesterol (milligrams)	Fat (grams)
Roasted Peanuts, 1 oz	165	0	14
Marshmallows, 3	60	0	0
Ice Cream Sandwich, 1	200	15	6
Gum, 1 stick	9	0	0
Granola Bar	130	2	4
Fudge, 1 oz	115	1	4
Donut, Chocolate, 1	330	20	13
Saltine Crakers, 4	50	4	1
Potato Chips, 1 oz	160	0	13
Corn Chips, 1 oz	150	0	9
Cheese Puffs, 1 oz	156	156	10
Chocolate Bar, 1 oz	160	7	8
Pecans	190	0	18
Popsicle	70	0	0
Popcorn, salt and butter, 1 c	40	6	3
Pretzels, 10 small sticks	10	0	trace
Sunflower seeds, 1 oz	165	0	14

Antioxidants, Cholesterol & Heart Disease

SOUPS	Calories	Cholesterol	Fat
		(milligrams)	(grams)
Vegetable, 1 cup	80	0	2
Tomato, 1 cup	100	0	2
Split Pea, 1 cup	190	3	3
Minestrone, 1 cup	83	3	3
Creamed, most kinds, 1 cup	135	20	7
Clam Chowder, 1 cup	80	2	2
Chili with meat, 1 cup	170	12	8
Chicken Noodle, 1 cup	75	5	2
Beef Noodle, 1 cup	84	5	3
Bean and Bacon, 1 cup	170	3	6

VEGETABLES	Calories	Cholesterol	Fat
		(milligrams)	(grams)
Tomato, 1 medium	40	0	trace
Spinach, 1 cup	40	0	trace
Canned peas, 1 cup	140	0	trace
Canned mushrooms, 1 cup	40	0	trace
Canned corn, 1 cup	170	0	2
Fresh Corn, 1 ear	70	0	1
Cauliflower, 1 cup	25	0	trace
Cooked carrots, 1 cup	45	0	trace
Raw Carrots, 1	20	0	trace
Cooked broccoli, 1 cup	40	0	trace
Green Beans, 1 cup	30	0	trace
Lima Beans, 1 cup	200	0	trace
Beans with Pork, 1 cup	280	18	4
Asparagus, 1 cup	35	0	2

FAST FOOD	Calories	Cholesterol	Fat
		(milligrams)	(grams)
Soft Shell Taco	186	21	10
Pepperoni Pizza, 1 slice	368	54	21
Chocolate Milk Shake, 10 oz	350	37	11
Cheese Burger	317	48	15

Antioxidants, Cholesterol & Heart Disease

Hamburger	269	33	12
French Fries, Regular	220	14	13
Fish Sandwich	470	90	27
Beef Burito	392	56	14

HOW DO I INCREASE MY INTAKE OF COMPLEX CARBOHYDRATES AND DIETARY FIBER?

Studies from various parts of the world has shown that people who consume foods that are rich of fruits, vegetables, whole grains, and legumes have decreased atherosclerosis. This is probably due to the low fat and cholesterol content, both of which are risk factors for heart disease. Some components of plant foods, such as soluble fiber and vegetable proteins may also contribute to this positive effect. A decreased fat diet with a combination of foods that are rich in soluble fiber can help reduce LDL cholesterol levels. Foods that are rich in soluble fiber are oatmeal, oatbran, apples, citrus fruits, strawberries, split peas, lentils, dried beans. It is recommended that a person consumes between 25 to 35 grams of fiber per day from a variety of sources. Also, the intake of complex carbohydrates should be increased to six or more servings per day. This should include a combination of breads, cereals, and legumes. As mentioned previously, it is important to read labels and fully understand their meaning. For example, a popular advertising idea is the phrase "contains fiber". Be cautioned! It is important to consider the quantity of fiber to which the advertisement refers. For example, if a product contains 2 grams of fiber, it can be labelled as a "source of fiber". If it contains 4 grams of fiber, it can be called a "high source of fiber" and if it contains 6 grams of fiber, it can be labelled a "very high source of fiber."

It is suggested that more than 55% of a person's carbohydrates (starches, vegetables, legumes, breads, cereals, and some fruits.) that are high in fat and high in sugar (e.g. desserts, baked goods) are the primary culprits for high calories. Furthermore, foods high in sugar content represent empty calories with little nutritive value.

It is important to recognize that meat and dairy products are not sources of fiber. Listed on the following page are some of the best sources of dietary fiber and their fiber content.

SOURCES OF DIETARY FIBER AND THEIR FIBER CONTENT

QUANTITY	PRODUCT	AMOUNT OF FIBER
1 cup (250 ml)	oatmeal cereal	3.0 gms
1 cup (250 ml)	oatbran cereal	4.0 gms
8 medium	strawberries	4.0 gms
1 cup	kidney beans	6.0 gms
1 cup	split-peas	4.5 gms
1 cup	baked beans	8.0 gms
2 tbsp	peanut butter	2.5 gms
1/2 cup	peanuts	4.0 gms
1/2 cup	all bran cereal	10.0 gms
1 slice	whole wheat bread	2.0 gms
1 small	bran muffin	3.0 gms
1/2 cup	brown rice	1.5 gms
1 cup	whole wheat pasta	4.5 gms

ARE THERE ANY FOODS WHICH I COULD EAT WHICH ACT AS ANTIOXIDANTS?

Vitamin E was discovered in 1922 but it wasn't accepted as a necessary requirement for humans until continuing evidence surfaced 40 years later. Vitamin E is required for most animal species including humans. Vitamin E is present in two forms found in plant materials. The most important group is the tocopherols, the other group is the tocotrienols. It is possible to synthesize vitamin E in laboratories. Synthesized vitamin E can be recognized by having the label dl-α-tocopherol. An example is Life brand vitamin E. The non-synthetic or natural form is designated d-α-tocopherol. The natural version of vitamin E is thought to have a higher activity than the synthetic form, presumably due to better absorption characteristics from the gastrointestinal tract into the blood stream. There are many different types of natural vitamin E. It is suggested that the bioavailability of clear base vitamin E is greater than its counterparts. An example of this is Natural Factors Clear Base vitamin E.

The Vitamin E content of foods varies greatly depending on storage, processing

DIETARY SOURCES OF VITAMIN E

Vegetable oils

(wheatgerm,safflower,cottonseed, soybean, sunflower)

Whole grains

Nuts

(walnuts, filberts, pecans, almonds)

Dry Beans

Brown Rice

Sweet Potatoes

Seeds

(sunflower, sesame, pumpkin)

Dark Green Leafy Vegetables

and food preparation procedures. Most North Americans get the largest amount of vitamin E from food oils (such as soybean, corn, sunflower) and products made from these oils (like shortening and margarine). However, it is not recommended to consume large amounts of these products because of the high amount of fatty acids that they contain. Meats, fish, animal fats, and most fruits and vegetables have very little vitamin

Antioxidants, Cholesterol & Heart Disease

E.   Green   leafy   vegetables   supply appreciable amounts of this nutrient. It is recommended that one consumes five or more servings of a variety of vegetables and fruits, especially green and yellow vegetables and citrus fruits.

Vitamin C is another commonly available antioxidant.   Although it can act as an antioxidant at high concentrations, it also acts as a pro-oxidant at low concentrations. The capacity of vitamin C to reduce the risk of heart disease is currently controversial. Two recent studies published in the New England Journal of Medicine involving thousands of people in the United States reported no association of vitamin C with a lower risk of heart disease. However, these data were at odds with another study published   in   the   scientific   journal Epidemiology which did show a protective action of vitamin C.   It is reasonable to conclude at this point that the jury is still out on the issue. We do know that several animal   species   exhibit   greater atherosclerotic development in their arteries when maintained on a marginally deficient diet of vitamin C for long periods of time. It has been thought that vitamin C may act as an antioxidant in conjunction with the more potent vitamin E. It may "spare" the vitamin E whenever the body comes under oxidative attack. The vitamin C may be used up first before the vitamin E. Thus, the protection afforded by the two antioxidants may be additive. However, this needs to be investigated further.

From a nutritional standpoint, supplementation of your diet with vitamin C may not be necessary. A person can achieve very high levels of vitamin C in the blood simply by ingesting food rich in C. This is not the case for vitamin E. High levels of vitamin E in the blood can be reached only through consuming vitamin E supplements. Foods do not contain enough E for one to realistically expect to elevate their blood concentrations substantially.

FOOD SOURCES OF VITAMIN C

Type	Quantity	Amount
Broccoli	1/2 cup	37
Brussels Sprouts	1/2 cup	35
Cabbage, Raw	1 cup	33
Cantaloupe	1/2 med	195
Cauliflower, Raw	1/2 cup	36
Grapefruit	1 med	100
Green Pepper	1/2 cup	45
Kiwi Fruit	1 med	74
Mango	1 med	57
Orange	1 med	70
Papaya	1 cup	87
Red Pepper	1/2 cup	95
Strawberries	1 cup	84
Sweet Potato	1 small	31
Tomato	1 cup	34
Watermelon	1 slice	46

Antioxidants, Cholesterol & Heart Disease

Another potentially important antioxidant is coenzyme Q10. Coenzyme Q10, also called ubiquinone, is a vitamin-like essential substance that acts as a natural antioxidant. Like vitamin E, coenzyme Q10 is carried in the blood associated with LDL. It is also found in cell membranes and any other place in the body where fat is deposited. Various scientific studies have shown that coenzyme Q10 may posess beneficial properties that help the heart function properly. The concentration of coenzyme Q10 found in the hearts of patients suffering from heart failure is lower than that of their healthier counterparts. In a study involving humans, it was shown that patients suffering from congestive heart failure had a significant reduction in hospitalization, better stabilization of their heart failure, and fewer incidences of serious complications when they took coenzyme Q10 in addition to their conventional thearpy. Increases in body stores of coenzyme Q10 can be achieved by the use of oral supplementation of coenzyme Q10 (100mg per day). Vita Health is an example of a suitable brand of coenzyme Q10 supplement which is available in most drug and health food stores.

Foods which contain antioxidants are relatively easy to find. If you know which foods contain vitamin E, vitamin C or beta carotene, then you are able to select those foods which contain antioxidants. However, you may be surprised by some foods which do contain antioxidants, so a listing of these foods is found below.

FOOD SOURCES OF ANTIOXIDANTS

Avocado	Mango
Blueberries	Papaya
Broccoli	Peaches
Brussel Sprouts	Pumpkin
Cabbage	Purple Grapes
Cantaloupe	Raspberries
Carrots	Red Peppers
Cherries	Spinach
Chili Peppers	Spirulina
Citrus Fruits	Squash
Cranberries	Strawberries
Green Tea	Sweet Potatoes
Kale	Tomatoes
Kiwi	Turnip Greens

Antioxidants, Cholesterol & Heart Disease

THE END

Antioxidants, Cholesterol & Heart Disease

APPENDIX

SUGGESTED READING

1. "Cholesterol and Atherosclerosis" by Scott M. Grundy, Gower Medical Publishing, New York, NY, 1990.
2. "Brand Name: Fat and Cholesterol Counter" by the American Heart Association, Times Books, NY, 1994.
3. "The Complete Vitamin Book" by Carl Lowe, Berkeley Books, NY, 1994.
4. "The Antioxidant Vitamin Counter" by AB Natow & J-A Heslin, Pocket Books, NY, 1994.

Antioxidants, Cholesterol & Heart Disease

INDEX

brain, 28, 63
bran, 106, 135

C

calories, 92, 94, 115, 116, 117, 124, 134
cancer, 9, 106
cardiovascular disease, 9, 13, 35, 51
carrots, 76, 131
cell membrane, 29, 139
cells, 28, 31, 38, 47, 56, 58, 60, 63, 67, 69, 71, 72, 74, 80, 96, 99, 105
chest pain, 54, 59, 62, 82, 90, 100
cholesterol, 10, 15, 16, 19, 21, 22, 23, 24, 27, 28, 31, 33, 34, 35, 36, 37, 38, 39, 41, 43,
    44, 53, 56, 57, 58, 59, 66, 67, 68, 71, 79, 80, 81, 85, 86, 90, 92, 93, 94, 95, 97, 98,
    99, 100, 101, 103, 104, 106, 108, 110, 112, 114, 115, 117, 119, 122, 124, 133, 142
cholesterol bad, 39
cholesterol blood, 16,22,34,41,54,86,90,92,95,98,99,102,104,106
cholesterol clearance, 95
cholesterol good, 40
cholesterol levels, 31, 33, 34, 37, 41, 67, 90, 92, 95, 96, 97, 98, 99, 101, 104
cholesterol and heart disease 12,34,66,69,78,86,104,106
cholestyramine, 98, 102
circulation, 39, 63, 96
clofibrate, 100
coconut oil, 104
coenzyme Q-10, 139
colestid, 98
colestipol, 98
compounds, 31, 75, 76, 83, 101
concentration, 16, 33, 37, 39, 54, 57, 68, 69, 72, 98, 101, 104, 139
cooking oil, 38, 92
coronary arteries, 58, 61
coronary artery disease, 10, 77, 89, 90

D

dairy products, 104
death, 9, 16, 35, 62, 63, 82, 106
diabetes, 45, 46, 100, 124
diet, 10, 23, 32, 81, 89, 92, 95, 98, 105
drugs, 23, 81, 97, 98, 99, 100, 101

E

endothelial cells, 72
environment, 29
exercise, 10, 23, 85, 86, 88, 108

F

fats, 23, 27, 38, 45, 71, 72, 75, 92, 94, 98, 103, 104, 117, 137
fatty acid, 103
fiber, 23, 24, 106, 111, 133, 134
fibers, 106
fibroblasts, 72
fish, 31, 114, 120, 123, 137
foam, 69, 73
foam cells, 69, 73
free radicals, 72, 74, 77, 78, 80, 81
fruits, 84, 114, 133, 134, 137

G

gallstones, 100
gemfibrozil, 100
genetics, 45, 53
ghee, 71

H

hardening of the arteries, 58
HDL, 39, 46, 79, 85, 100, 101, 108
heart, 5, 9, 17, 22, 28, 34, 39, 41, 43, 46, 48, 49, 50, 52, 53, 56, 58, 60, 63, 66, 67, 69, 77, 81, 89, 90, 94, 98, 99, 100, 101, 104
heart attack, 10, 17, 22, 23, 41, 45, 47, 48, 49, 50, 52, 53, 54, 59, 62, 63, 67, 89, 90
heart disease, 5, 9, 17, 22, 34, 39, 41, 43, 44, 46, 48, 50, 51, 53, 55, 56, 58, 59, 66, 68, 69, 77, 82, 83, 86, 89, 98, 100, 101, 104, 124, 133
heart failure, 10, 35, 51, 55
high density lipoprotein, 39
hormones, 28, 51
humans, 31
hypertension, 45, 108

T

V